# what is a pilgrimage?

A pilgrimage is a spiritual journey taken for the purpose of getting closer to God or to whatever you choose to call life's central mystery.

The idea of spiritual journeying is common to all humankind. Native Australians go Walkabout; Muslims make the hajj to Mecca; Christians go to Jerusalem, Rome, or Santiago de Compostela; Buddhists walk in their founder's footsteps. Hindus have such a vast choice of holy sites that it could take a lifetime to visit them all.

All pilgrimages are undertaken at a special time in a person's life—between college and work, for example, or after a bereavement. Pilgrimage is a time away from ordinary life, a time to look back, reflect, and assess all that has led up to this special moment.

A pilgrimage brings personal renewal. On the journey, pilgrims rediscover themselves and reaffirm their relationship with God. But every pilgrimage includes a return journey, when it is time to come back to the world—refreshed, joyful, and ready to flourish.

For mystics of all faiths, this outer journey is a metaphor for an inward pilgrimage—the soul's journey in search of the light within.

W0010066

*Leave righteous ways behind, not to speak of unrighteous ways.*

BUDDHA (GAUTAMA SIDDHARTHA)
(563–483BC)

Before you begin to use this book, it is important to clarify some of your own ideas.

Try answering these questions. Keep your responses brief—answer in point form, if you like.

*What does pilgrimage mean to you?*

*Why do you want to take this journey now? Do you feel you are ready for it?*

*Has anything happened to make you consider a pilgrimage?*

Traditionally, pilgrims left behind their worldly possessions, entrusting them to the safekeeping of a close friend. See this as a metaphor for leaving behind all the worldly things that annoy you right now. While you are using this book, try not to worry about problems concerning work, money, or relationships. Leave these cares behind and give yourself time out.

*What would you like to pack away for the time being and put in your metaphorical attic?*

*What do you expect to find at the end of your journey?*

When you have completed your inner pilgrimage, come back and read these answers.
You may be surprised how different you feel on your return.

## what to pack ...

You are going on a journey, so you need to pack your bags with
a few essentials. Here are some things to take with you.

### Stamina
You may find your determination to complete the journey faltering,
and there are bound to be times when you need to push yourself.

### Trust
To achieve successful results from your pilgrimage, it is crucial to
maintain trust in yourself and trust in the process.

### Imagination
You will be asked to exercise your imagination—often—so don't
forget to bring it with you.

### Rhythm
Imagine that you are walking along the pilgrim's road. Your feet are
repeatedly hitting a dirt track. You have many miles to go, so you
need to build up a rhythm—a heartbeat—to keep going.

### A sense of humor
Most of the pilgrimage is supposed to be fun, so don't waste energy
being too earnest.

## ... and what to leave behind

You will eventually need to leave behind most things, including your preconceptions, prejudices, self-doubt, and fears. But no one expects you to do that immediately—you will probably shed them gradually as you go along your path.

Nevertheless, before you shut the front door and turn the key in the lock, you should really set aside some time to spring-clean your home, take out the garbage, and clear up your affairs. Nobody wants to come back home to a mess.

**Before you start the pilgrimage:**
• Make sure you are up to date with all your bills and paperwork. You don't want to interrupt the pilgrimage to spend a weekend completing a tax return.
• Give your home a thorough clean and put away clutter. This is the space where you are going to be doing a lot of your imagining, so it needs to be calm.
• If possible, create a particular spot in your home where you can write your journal and dream the pilgrim's dream.
• Tie up loose ends at work—you don't want to bring problems home with you, much less on a pilgrimage.
• Make a list of all the problems involving relationships and emotions that are bothering you at the present time. Put the list in a box—and forget about it.

# cleansing meditation

Use this meditation whenever you feel life is getting on top of you.
See it as a way of flushing out bad energy.

**The breath of life**
Sit cross-legged on a cushion on the floor or upright in a chair with
both feet on the ground. Sit up straight and feel each vertebra in
your spine in alignment and your skull balanced on top.

Take deep breaths through your nose. Either close your eyes or
focus on a spot in the middle distance. Feel the breath right down
to your pelvis as you breathe in, and pouring right through your
body as you breathe out. Concentrate on your breathing. Let your
stomach bulge on the in breath and collapse on the out breath.
Continue breathing like this for the rest of the meditation.

Imagine a cord of colored lights running down your spine from
your skull and into the ground—from the end of your spine if you
are cross-legged or the soles of your feet if you are sitting. Keep
breathing. Imagine bad energy draining out of the cord. Then
imagine a shaft of white light above your head pouring into your
body and down your spine, down your arms to your hands, out
of your hands, through your torso, and pushing the colored lights
out into the ground. You are pushing all the bad energy out of
your body and replacing it with cleansing white light.

Stay with this light for as long as you like. When you are ready
to stop, let the light spin in a whirlpool just above your heart. Allow
it to get smaller and smaller. When it is a tiny dot, breathe it into
your heart and out of your mouth in a sharp exhalation.

*Open your eyes and feel fresh.*

## your body is going on a journey, too

One of the consequences of taking a pilgrimage on foot—as was traditional in medieval Europe, for example—is that you would come home ultra-fit, having shed any excess pounds and built up a lithe, muscular body. Walking ten or more miles a day in the fresh air was bound to turn even the chubbiest friar into a leaner, younger-feeling version of himself.

**Exercise**

Try to exercise for at least twenty minutes a day during your inner pilgrimage. Work up a sweat. The hormones released in exercise are the best natural medicine against depression.

**Food**

Enjoy your food during this time and attempt to eat healthily. You could imagine that your pilgrimage is in Spain or India and try out dishes from those countries. But don't embark on a weight-loss diet or any other regime unless it's already a permanent part of your life. One set of disciplines at a time is enough.

**Sunshine**

Get outside as much as possible. Sunshine is good for you. Even if there is no sun where you are, clouds can be beneficial, too. Breathe in natural, clean air as often and as regularly as you can.

*If anything is sacred, the*
*human body is sacred.*

WALT WHITMAN (1819–92),
I SING THE BODY ELECTRIC

# open your spirit

An inner pilgrimage is about allowing yourself to feel the positive energy of the earth and everything in it. It is about letting go of negative thought patterns, old neuroses, and bad habits. To achieve this, you need to be able to open your spirit. This is often a gradual process that gets easier as the pilgrimage progresses. Meanwhile, here are a few ideas you should consider taking on your journey.

### Prayer and meditation

When the mind is calm, the spirit opens up. Try allowing your mind to empty and your spirit to open first thing every morning. You may choose to say a traditional prayer, practice yoga, or even sing. Just do what feels right for you. Keeping the pilgrim's journal should also be a form of meditation.

### Living in the now

Zen Buddhists believe that being able to live in the now is the closest we can get to bliss. If we give ourselves up completely to performing even the smallest action—chopping vegetables, putting on socks, answering the telephone—with all of our focus, then we are getting close to a state of peace. This does not mean switching off and zoning out as you chop up the onion, but focusing, enjoying, and feeling that moment completely. People with absorbing hobbies will find it easy to recognize this state.

Very few people can do this all the time—and, frankly, it's not advisable to wander around in a Zen state in the modern world. But try to focus like this, concentrating yourself on being in the moment, at least once a day.

## Visualization

The ability to use your imagination is essential if you want to make a success of your inner pilgrimage. Visualization is one of the most powerful tools you have for exploring your inner world. Some people—dreamers—find that visualization is a cinch. Others have to work hard at it.

If you get into the habit of practicing visualization every day, you will find that it gradually gets easier. A good time to do it is on the way into work if you travel by public transportation, or while taking a walk in the park, for example.

Every day imagine the landscape of this stage of your pilgrimage. Are you walking on a narrow path through high mountains today? Or are you walking along a broad grassy track through fields of wild flowers?

Write down what you see each day in your pilgrim's journal—and you will find that your visualization tells a story all its own.

*To see a World in a grain of sand*
*And a Heaven in a wild flower*
*Hold Infinity in the palm of your hand,*
*And Eternity in an hour.*

WILLIAM BLAKE (1757–1827),
AUGURIES OF INNOCENCE

# the spiritual spiral

Since this is your inner pilgrimage, you need to think about your own faith—or lack of it—as you start out on your journey. Try this simple exercise to see how far your faith has brought you up to this moment in your life. In the center of a sheet of paper, draw a large spiral. Leave room at the top and bottom of the page to write.

Imagine the spiral as a timeline that starts with your birth at the center and ends with yourself as you are now. Identify spiritual turning points and write them in at the appropriate place. Then use the space above and below the spiral to annotate each event, focusing on your experience of faith, rather than on general life experience. If you need more room, continue on another page.

**examples of spiritual turning points**

*5 years: the first time I felt aware of life's mystery (seeing a bee in a flower)*

*6 years: the day I lost my teddy (and understood death)*

*19 years: the first time I fell in love*

*25 years: my age when my mother died*

*27 years: the time of my conversion*

*34 years: the birth of my child*

As you work on the spiral, you will be surprised at how many spiritual ups and downs you have already had. Most people go through periods of faith and loss of faith. The older you are, the more likely there are to be patterns in your spiritual life.

You can keep the completed spiral in the pocket at the beginning of this chapter and take it out whenever you want to remind yourself of your spiritual journey.

# the pilgrim's journal

It may take a while to get into the swing of the pilgrim's journal—
after all, this is an exercise that can be pretty demanding on the
imagination—but you can put as much or as little effort into each
page as you like. Here are two sample entries to get you going.

**first example**

*On the way to work, I found myself remembering the precise feeling of being small on
a crowded bus. The claustrophobia, the size of people's shoes! I remember my hand
enfolded in my mother's, so safe. That feeling of total trust and safety is something
I look for—all the time. But it occurs to me now that perhaps I've been looking in the
wrong places. Maybe it's myself that I don't trust.*

*Bought a balloon on the way back from work. Felt silly trailing through the park
with it, but after I got home spent a good twenty minutes bouncing it off the ceiling.
Feeling light as air, mindless, full of delight.*

**second example**

*This is the beautiful landscape I visualized today. I am in a shallow, sunlit valley with
a stream and a footpath running through high grass. I feel curious, elated. I see tiny
flowers and colorful butterflies. There is a rowan tree by a boulder. The journey is easy.
I am gently climbing up, but with an easy swinging pace. I am excited and can't wait to
see what lies in the next valley.*

## rediscovering your lost innocence

As we grow from child to adult, we develop a shell of protection to deal with the rigors of life. This is as it should be. But sometimes that shell begins to take over our entire personality, and we forget about the tender, sensitive person that we carry within.

You may want to think of this person as your "inner child," someone as innocent as you used to be, but at the same time as wise as you have become. This wise child is here to accompany you on your pilgrimage, to help you experience the world with fresh eyes.

Your childhood may have been a golden time or a period of suffering, or—as it was for most people—a bit of both. Whatever it was, you experienced the world with an intensity and a directness that are hard to recapture as an adult.

In this stage of the journey, you will seek out that inner child, allow him or her to speak to you, hold your hand, and guide you along the way. You may find this process makes you feel more vulnerable—so clothe yourself with a little bit of adult armor before venturing out into the world.

*We'll talk of sunshine and of song,*
*And summer days, when we were young;*
*Sweet childish days, that were as long*
*As twenty days are now.*

WILLIAM WORDSWORTH (1770–1850),
TO A BUTTERFLY

## remembering yourself as a child

You may find it helpful to repeat the following exercise at regular intervals during this stage of the journey.

**A childhood memory**
Start by finding a comfortable place to sit, or lie on your back on the floor or a bed. Close your eyes and concentrate on taking in long, deep breaths through your nose. When you feel relaxed, imagine a cool white light in the center of your forehead, bathing your brain in light. Enjoy that feeling.

Now allow a happy moment from your childhood to enter your inner vision. You may well be flooded with a jumble of memories. Try singling one out to re-live and enjoy.

When you have finished, let the white light return and slowly let it drain out through your fingers and toes back into the earth.

Now—while the feeling is still in your head and heart—write about it.

*What was the memory? How did you feel emotionally and physically?*

*... The childhood shows the man,*
*As morning shows the day.*

JOHN MILTON (1608–74), PARADISE REGAINED

Collect pictures of what you consider to be a happy childhood and glue them to these pages.

They may be images of your own childhood—or of the childhood you wish you'd had.

## the pilgrim's journal

During this stage of the journey, see the world with the fresh eyes
of a child. Try to experience the world as if it were all new.

**How to use the journal**
The journal works on two levels—in your daily life and in your
imagination. You can use it as you would a normal diary, to keep
a record of your life ... but you can also imagine that each page
of the journal is one stage of a long journey on foot to a site of
special significance to you.

  Describe how you are feeling emotionally and spiritually. On
some pages, you may feel moved to write an imaginary account
of a day—on others, you may want to write about real life. But
don't waste space complaining about colleagues or your broken
dishwasher (unless you feel that in some way these form part
of your journey). This is a journal about your inner state. Pay
attention to living in the moment and see how that feels.

  Treat the "task" on each page as inspiration rather than
direction. This is not a checklist. But you may want to do the
tasks more than once—they are supposed to be fun.

**While you are on your pilgrimage:**
• Take some exercise every day.
• Eat food you like.
• Take a little time every day to clear your mind.
• Keep your spirit open to chance.
• Exercise your imagination.

Go a different way to work this morning or vary a route that you often take—and look around you.

*What did you see on your new route? Did you overhear any funny or interesting conversations?*

*Did you smell any new smells?*

Cook yourself your favorite childhood meal—spaghetti hoops, alphabet soup, or toasted marshmallows, for example. Eat all of it by yourself. Consider what the experience means to you and what memories it evokes.

Are you sitting comfortably? Then move to a place where you've never sat before—under the table, on the kitchen counter, behind the television.

*What's the view like from there?*

Buy yourself a balloon—and play with it, either on your own or with one or two children.

Imagine that you are the balloon.

*What's its personality?*

Examine the immediate area around your home in minute detail. Look at every crack in the sidewalk and every leaf on every tree.

*Have you seen anything new?*

Take yourself to see a children's movie or rent your favorite one on video or DVD. Kick back and enjoy it with all your heart. You don't need to write a film review here—or anything at all—but you may want to recall the excitement of your first time at the movies.

*A child's world is fresh and new and beautiful, full of wonder and excitement. It is our misfortune that for most of us that clear-eyed vision, that true instinct for what is beautiful and awe-inspiring, is dimmed and even lost before we reach adulthood.*

RACHEL CARSON (1907–64), THE SENSE OF WONDER

Smile at a stranger—and make eye contact. Whatever reaction you get, remain calm and let the experience wash over you.

*When was the last time you did that? Would you do it more often?*

You have been on your journey several days now. You are beginning to develop a rhythm as you walk.
Imagine meeting a small man in a red cap. He has a little dog with him and a face full of merriment.
*What does he say to you?*

*"A child of five would understand this.*
*Send somebody to fetch a child of five."*

GROUCHO MARX (1895–1977), DUCK SOUP

Did you have an imaginary friend when you were little? If you didn't, invent one now and let him or her hang around for a while.

*Who was your imaginary friend? What did you talk about?*

Get a fit of the giggles—by hook or by crook. Do whatever it takes—sit on a whoopee cushion, allow someone to tickle you, read Dave Barry or P. G. Wodehouse.

*How does that feel?*

*What three gifts did your fairy godmother give you at birth?*

*If I had influence with the good fairy who is supposed to preside over the christening of all children, I should ask that her gift to each child in the world be a sense of wonder so indestructible that it would last throughout life.*

RACHEL CARSON (1907–64), THE SENSE OF WONDER

*What were your three favorite toys as a child? Do you remember why?*

Put some music on and dance like a child—freely, madly—stamp your feet, wave your arms in the air. Spin around until you are dizzy.

*Do you feel happier? Should you dance more often?*

Imagine sitting on a grassy hillock in the warm midmorning sun. Around you are wild flowers and before you a wonderful view. You spy a figure coming along the path. It is a small child. It is you.

*What do you say to each other?*

## connecting with nature

By now you should be getting used to writing about your feelings and keeping the journal regularly. You should be enjoying yourself—and your step should be a little lighter. The child you met on the last stage of the journey has led you along the pilgrim's way to this point—where the path forks and you need to make a choice.

You can take the easy route down, back into your safe, old way of life, and see this last stage as a little detour—or you can take the other route, less traveled, more intriguing, maybe into a region where you could meet lions and tigers and bears.

On the less traveled path, you may be sleeping outdoors—it's rough, it's exciting, it's nature in the raw. By getting closer to nature, you will be coming closer to the central mystery of life.

Even if you live in the middle of a concrete jungle, nature is everywhere—in the play of clouds overhead, in the shoots of grass struggling through the gaps in the paving slabs, in the wind against your cheek, and in the sun through your window.

If you are fortunate enough to live surrounded by nature unadorned, this is your chance to revel in it without restraint.

*Go where he will, the wise man is at home,*
*His hearth the earth, his hall the azure dome.*

RALPH WALDO EMERSON (1803–82), WOODNOTES

Use these pages to collect images of landscapes, plants, and animals that you find awesome, inspiring, or beautiful. Maybe you will encounter some of them on this stage of the journey.

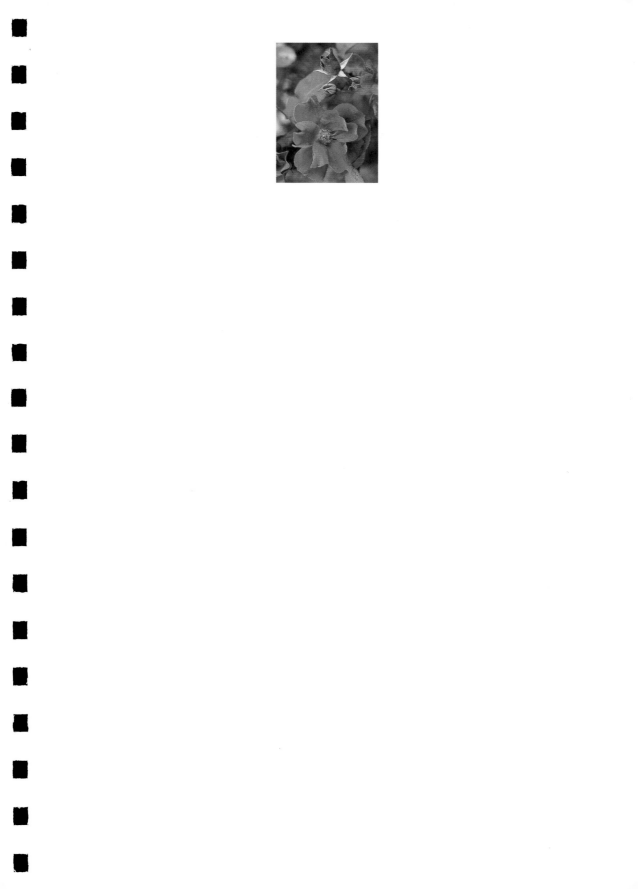

Make a list of all the natural wonders you have ever wanted to see.

*What makes you want to see them? How do you think you would feel?*

Make a life plan for encountering the natural wonders that attract you most. For example,

the Grand Canyon—by the time I'm 42.

# the pilgrim's journal

During this stage of the journey, appreciate the wonders of nature wherever you look. Remember that you, too, are part of the natural world; your body is one of God's miracles. The people around you, no matter how hard they try to hide it, are also part of that world.

**While you are on your pilgrimage:**
• Take some exercise every day—and during this stage try to do it outdoors. Spend as much time as you can outside.
• Eat food you like—and on this stage try eating as much raw and unprocessed food as you can tolerate. Savor its freshness.
• Take a little time every day to clear your mind.
• Keep your spirit open to chance.
• Exercise your imagination.

*Glory be to God for dappled things—*
*For skies of couple-colour as a brinded cow;*
*For rose-moles all in stipple upon trout that swim;*
*Fresh-firecoal chestnut-falls; finches' wings;*
*Landscape plotted and pieced—fold, fallow, and plough;*
*And all trades, their gear and tackle and trim.*

*All things counter, original, spare, strange;*
*Whatever is fickle, freckled (who knows how?)*
*With swift, slow; sweet, sour; adazzle, dim;*
*He fathers-forth whose beauty is past change:*
*Praise him.*

GERARD MANLEY HOPKINS (1844–89), PIED BEAUTY

Go for a walk today. *Anywhere*. Find a perfect leaf and treasure it between these pages.

Get up before dawn and find a perch from which to watch the miracle of sunrise. If you can't do it today, do it tomorrow. Let the sight suffuse you with joy. Allow yourself to savor it slowly, solitarily. Hear it, smell it, feel it, see it ... write about it now.

Spend today thinking about smells. Consider all the smells you encounter in a day—coffee, soap, sweat. Try to describe them exactly.

*Do any of them have particular emotional effects?*

Go to the park or wander through the great outdoors and find a tree that you like. Discover the tree's personality. Touch it, lean against it, look up into its branches, spend an hour or two near it. Write about it.

*Trees are poems that the earth writes upon the sky.*

KAHLIL GIBRAN (1883–1931), SAND AND FOAM

Eat fruit that is in season and think about how it connects you with nature.

*What are the sounds of nature that you hear every day?*

Imagine that you are walking through a sun-speckled wood and you come across a pregnant woman sitting in a glade. She is beautiful with skin like petals and shining eyes. She beckons you to sit beside her as she contemplates the beauty of the sun in the trees.

*What does she say to you?*

Collect a pebble today, wash it under running water, dry it carefully, and keep it in your pocket. Whenever you become aware of the pebble, touch it and remember than you are making contact with the earth.

*What does this mean to you?*

*For many years I was self-appointed inspector of snow-storms and rain-storms and did my duty faithfully.*

HENRY DAVID THOREAU (1817–62), WALDEN

If it is summertime, walk barefoot on grass. If there is snow lying on the ground, make a snow-angel. If it is cold and wet, splash in a puddle. Write about how it feels.

_____

_____

_____

_____

_____

_____

_____

_____

_____

_____

_____

_____

_____

_____

_____

_____

_____

Using as many similes and metaphors as you can, describe the life of a butterfly.

*In what way is the butterfly's life a metaphor for other things?*

*As kingfishers catch fire, dragonflies
draw flame ...*

GERARD MANLEY HOPKINS (1844–89)

Pick or buy a flower. Take it home with you and look at it in detail.

*What colors can you see? How does it smell? What texture are the petals?*

*Rosebush, I have come a sweet
springtide unto you, to seize you
very gently in my embrace.*

Mowlana Jalaluddin Rumi (1207–73)

Look out of your window and study the sky. Describe what you see.

Imagine that you are walking slowly across a desert plain. In the far distance you can see blue mountains. All around you there are perfect ridges of sand and thorn trees. You come across a cactus, and as you watch, it bursts into flower. Out of the flower a tiny woman appears. She is as perfect and delightful as a ballerina. She leaps nimbly onto your hand.

*What does she say to you?*

## entering the slough of despond

How is the inside of your head now? One aim of an inner pilgrimage is to allow yourself to open up spiritually, to gain the confidence to become more experimental and carefree. So far, you should have had plenty of fun indulging your creative imagination.

But around this time, just before the halfway mark in your pilgrimage, you may have reached a stage where you are assailed by self-doubt. It may occur to you that this is a dumb thing to be doing—a self-indulgent and childish exercise. What kind of a fool are you to think you even deserve to go on a pilgrimage, inner or outer?

Well, so it may be. Instead of ignoring those doubts—and letting them come up and grab you later—indulge them. Haul them out from the cellar, acknowledge them, analyze them. Try to figure out their origins.

Ask this question: what are you afraid of finding out about yourself if you carry on down the pilgrim's rocky pathway?

*The name of the slough was Despond. Here, therefore, they wallowed for a while being grievously bedaubed with the dirt; and Christian, because of the burden that was on his back, began to sink in the mire.*

John Bunyan (1628–88),
The Pilgrim's Progress

Make a list of all the reasons why you should take the next flight home.

| Doubt | Reasoning | What's it really about? |
| --- | --- | --- |
| | | |
| | | |
| | | |
| | | |
| | | |
| | | |
| | | |
| | | |
| | | |
| | | |
| | | |
| | | |
| | | |
| | | |
| | | |
| | | |
| | | |
| | | |

## your shadow

In all of us there is a darkness or a shadow. Although we would like to keep it buried in the cellar, sometimes it just won't stay down. It comes out unexpectedly in our dreams, in our behavior, and even in the people we meet and the situations in which we find ourselves. (Do you have a "friend" you can't stand? That's one manifestation of your shadow.) Our darkness may come to us as shameful or hurtful memories.

Remember that nobody's perfect. We have all done dumb, cruel—even destructive—things. We have all suffered from the actions of others. And sometimes you have got to forgive yourself for your past misdemeanors and mistakes, and move on. If you cannot do anything to fix 'em, leave 'em. Look at them now, allow yourself some wallowing time, and then let go. Hanging on to guilt is eventually sheer self-indulgence.

It is time also to forgive those you believe have harmed you. If you just cannot forgive, bear in mind that holding on to your anger damages you, consumes your energy. It does not heal. Examine the people and behavior that hurt you. Then put them away. You are on your pilgrimage now.

During this stage of the journey, try walking with your shadow—enlist its help. Let it change shape whenever it wants, and record the changes—they may give you a lot of insight.

Name your worst character traits. To get you started, consider the seven deadly sins: pride, covetousness, lust, envy, gluttony, anger, and sloth. Have you committed any of these? In what circumstances? Or is there anything else about your character that needs addressing? Use the first column to describe the trait and what you think has caused it. In the second column write down how you could change your behavior for the better.

By changing our outward behavior, we can gradually change how we feel inside.

| Bad trait | What I can do to change it |
| --- | --- |
| | |
| | |
| | |
| | |
| | |
| | |
| | |
| | |
| | |
| | |
| | |
| | |
| | |
| | |

Life hurts a lot less if we can accept our flaws. Most of us have a tendency to exaggerate those things about ourselves that are less than perfect, and there are many words that we use to express our weaknesses: cowardice, self-hatred, selfishness, lack of self-control, laziness, prejudice ...

But sometimes we may be able to find hidden in weakness a secret seed of goodness. Taking that seed and allowing it to flourish is part of the pilgrim's way. For example, if one of your weaknesses is cowardice, you may feel that you never stand up for yourself or for other people—but this trait probably makes you a good peace broker.

Choose one weakness and write about how it might be turned into a strength.

*What in me is dark*
*Illumine, what is low raise and support.*

JOHN MILTON (1608–74), PARADISE LOST, BOOK I

## the pilgrim's journal

During this stage of the journey, you are entering the dark. You may be traveling by night for some of the time. You may not like some of the things you see, for there are lions and tigers and bears in these woods. But when you have come through to the other side, you will be stronger and more at peace with yourself.

**While you are on your pilgrimage:**
• Take some exercise every day.
• Eat food you like—and during this stage, try some food you thought you'd never like.
• Take a little time every day to clear your mind—this is especially important now.
• Keep your spirit open to chance—pay special attention to the way you feel about the people you come across every day. Notice good and bad reactions, and ask yourself what has prompted these reactions.
• Exercise your imagination—read some fairy tales and think about their darker side.

*I have a little shadow that goes in and out with me,*
*And what can be the use of him is more than I can see.*
*He is very, very like me from the heels up to the head;*
*And I see him jump before me, when I jump into my bed.*

Robert Louis Stevenson (1850–94), My Shadow

Imagine that you are walking in a snowy landscape. You see the footprints of an animal. You follow them a little while and suddenly you see ...

Go out for a meal by yourself—go somewhere you have never been before.

*Was it easy? How conspicuous did you feel?*

Write a fairy story featuring these elements: a monster, a death, a magical object. If you need more space for your story, use some extra paper.

It is no good casting out devils.
They belong to us, we must
accept them and be at peace
with them.

D.H. Lawrence (1885–1930),
Phoenix, "The Reality of Peace"

Is there anything about yourself you are really ashamed of? Are you right to feel shame? If so, is there anything you can do to put things right? If not, promise yourself not to carry the burden any longer.

Carry a stone with you for a day and a night. Imagine the stone is a terrible burden—it represents the weight of all your guilt and anxiety. It is so heavy. Bury the stone.

Can you name one of your inner demons? Invite the demon to sit down in a chair opposite you and have a conversation. Ask the demon why it keeps bothering you.

Think about any irrational fears or phobias you may have. *What causes them?*

*Fear has many eyes and can see things underground.*

MIGUEL DE CERVANTES (1547–1616), DON QUIXOTE

Name your deepest secret. Do you really need to hide it? Write it on a piece of paper and put it under a rock next time you go for a walk, or whisper it on the wind. Now it is gone.

*Why was it a secret?*

"Angels and ministers of grace defend us!
Be thou a spirit of health or goblin damned,
Bring with thee airs from heaven or blasts
    from hell,
Be thy intents wicked or charitable,
Thou comest in such a questionable shape
That I will speak to thee: I'll call thee Hamlet,
King, father, royal Dane: O, answer me!
Let me not burst in ignorance, but tell
Why thy canonized bones, hearsed in death,
Have burst their cerements."

WILLIAM SHAKESPEARE (1564–1616), HAMLET I.IV.

Imagine yourself at a high mountain pass. Wind whistles past you. You are alone when suddenly out of the snow a figure approaches. He is large and hairy—a wild man—strong. He looks you in the eye. *What does he say to you?*

Imagine you have stopped to rest a while by a cool, dark pool. The sky is the color of pewter and the landscape is black. On the horizon is one stunted tree. In the depths of the pool are shadows—indefinable, imprecise. Look long and hard.

*What is it that you see?*

You have been carrying an item that you thought was indispensable—an essential part of who you are, a way of protecting yourself from the rigors of the journey. What is it? Is it an attitude? Is it an umbrella? Is it a memory? Somewhere along the way you have lost it, but you can't remember where. *How do you feel?*

Darkness falls around you. *What and who are you left with?*

You are ready to leave some things behind. Put them beside the path and feel yourself become lighter.

*What are they?*

## getting in touch with spirit

You have come through the dark part of the journey and you feel in the flow. Your doubts have been laid to rest, and your goal is almost in sight. Now it is time simply to enjoy the ride. Look around you. One of the pleasures of travel—armchair or otherwise—is the way it makes you more acutely aware of the everyday world and, especially, of your responses to it.

Think about lying in bed at night surrounded by your things, perhaps beside your loved one. Think about the building or street in which you live, your neighbors, the great spread of humanity across the globe—conscious, aware of its own existence; loving, crying, making babies.

Then think of the great mass of nature, bubbling with life—the singing rain forests and the whispering seas; the march of ants, the leap of a cat, the tenderness of a doe. And here are you, in the middle of it all, tiny and insignificant. Yet conscious.

Think of the clear night sky—millions of stars, distant worlds spinning and spinning in eternal space. And here are you, in bed in the dark, thinking of it all. The universe is in your mind. Why are we conscious? This is a miracle surely.

Look around you and you will see that every day you are surrounded by miracles. Try making a list of some of the small miracles that have occurred to you in the past week.

## synchronicity and chance

Most weeks, we experience a coincidence or two. Usually we ignore them. Even the idea of coincidence is treated dismissively. But on this stage of the journey, you should pay attention to coincidence.

The idea of synchronicity, or meaningful coincidence, is a powerful one. In the mid-20th century, the Swiss psychoanalyst Carl Gustav Jung was trying to understand why the Chinese oracle *I Ching* seemed to work for him. *I Ching* is a book of advice. The inquirer asks a question and then, using a divining method that relies entirely on chance, finds an answer in the book. Jung was intrigued to find that the answers seemed to be surprisingly accurate. The only explanation he could offer was synchronicity: the idea that two things happening simultaneously—that is, the asking of the question and the divination—were connected in a meaningful way.

If you extrapolate this idea into ordinary life, you may find a pattern underlying your ordinary experience—a mysterious rhythm of coincidence, of chance encounters, and unlikely and interesting correspondences. Children often instinctively understand this. Approach synchronicity lightly, however. There is a fine line between being alive to mysterious patterns and superstition.

*Fortune, that favours fools.*

BEN JONSON (1572–1637), THE ALCHEMIST

# a journey around your body

You may have seen the movie *Fantastic Voyage*, in which a group of medics are miniaturized and injected into a human body. Well, this exercise is like that.

Lie or sit somewhere comfortable where you won't be disturbed. Take several slow, deep breaths to calm yourself. When you are ready, imagine pale pink light washing through your body from head to foot, spreading out through the ground and into the earth. Imagine the pink light slowly draining away and taking with it any negative emotions. Focus on your breathing. Feel each foot in turn.

Imagine that you are a small person inside your foot examining the ligaments, bones, tendons, muscles, and blood that make up your foot. You are in a beautiful, living, breathing body. Then imagine that you are traveling up your leg, but the inside of your leg is a river of light and you are gliding up this river with the current. You arrive at your torso, and inside is a vast and beautiful landscape of hills and trees. Above you, the sky is blue. Take some time to explore.

When you are ready to continue, travel into your head. Perch yourself on the inside of your skull and look around. Above is a starry night sky—vast and infinite. Below is a beautiful blue sea. On the horizon the sun is rising, spreading its rosy fingers through the sky. Maybe you feel like swimming over to the island in the distance or catching a ride on the sailboat going by. You decide.

When you have finished exploring, wash your body with light again, letting it drain away into the earth. Plan to eat something or go to sleep after this exercise because it can be pretty amazing.

## the pilgrim's journal

During this stage of the journey, you walk tall, loose-limbed, and free. You are strong in mind and body, and look forward to each day. Your goal is in sight, but you have still enough time to savor the journey for itself, to feel each step of the way. A pilgrim on the Camino de Santiago in Spain once explained that each step is a prayer. Make it so for you.

**While you are on your pilgrimage:**
• Take some exercise every day.
• Eat food you like.
• Take a little time every day to clear your mind.
• Keep your spirit open to chance—during this stage, pay special attention to coincidence.
• Exercise your imagination—allow yourself to daydream as much as possible. Try to take your pilgrimage in your mind every day.

*For we walk by faith, not by sight.*

II Corinthians 5:7

Imagine walking through a meadow with the noon sun beating down. You stop by a stream, take off your shoes, and dip your feet in the water. A fish nibbles your toes and lifts its head above the water. *What does it tell you?*

Name five mysterious things that have happened in your life. Think of coincidences, lucky meetings, moments of sudden bliss.

*Do you pay enough attention to these moments?*

Imagine the full moon setting on the western horizon and the sun starting to rise in the east.

*Which way do the shadows fall?*

Imagine a perfectly ordinary day—a day in which everything feels just right and goes right.

*Now live it.*

*Would to God that we might spend a single day really well!*

THOMAS À KEMPIS (C.1380–1471),
THE IMITATION OF CHRIST

Go to your nearest botanical garden or plant nursery. Find the most ancient-looking plant.

The oldest known living tree is said to be almost 5,000 years old—think about that.

Look around your home and contemplate your possessions.

*What gives you pleasure?*

*My mind to me a kingdom is.*
*Such perfect joy therein I find*
*That it excels all other bliss*
*That world affords or grows by kind.*

Sir Edward Dyer (1543–1607),
The Contented Mind

On the path you reach a bridge over a wide rushing river. In the middle of the bridge you meet a beautiful man or woman. The beautiful person takes you by the hand and draws you to the far bank, where you lie down together in long grass.

Make it your mission to create a happy memory today—for yourself or someone else. Plan it—but, if things don't turn out according to your plan, go with the flow. Remember that you are creating a memory.

Imagine that you have a guardian angel. Now ask the angel why you are worth taking care of.

*Faith consists in believing when it is beyond the power of reason to believe. For something to be believed, it is not enough for it to be possible.*

Voltaire (1694–1778), Questions sur l'Encyclopédie

Watch the sun set. Feel faith.

List five achievements of which you are proud—and say why. Give yourself a pat on the back.

Now think about the next five.

Imagine swimming in the cool water of a mountain lake. Far out in the lake you meet two mermaids.

*What do they say to you?*

*One is happy as a result of one's own efforts, once one knows the ingredients of happiness—simple tastes, a degree of courage, self-denial to a point, love of work, and, above all, a clear conscience. Happiness is no vague dream, I now feel certain of that.*

GEORGE SAND (1804–76), CORRESPONDENCE

Make something beautiful—a meal, a flower arrangement, a painting. Make sure it is something you can finish in a few hours.

*I am certain of nothing but the holiness of the heart's affections and the truth of imagination—what the imagination seizes as beauty must be truth—whether it existed before or not.*

JOHN KEATS (1795–1821),
LETTER TO BENJAMIN BAILEY, 22 NOVEMBER 1817

*What does faith mean to you?* Write a short poem or poetic motto that sums up your feelings.

Carry it with you.

# inner sanctum

The sanctuary is in your heart. Your Jerusalem, your Mecca, your Benares—these places of spirit are all within you, available to you when you need solace and refreshment. Your inner pilgrimage has brought you here—to the light within. Take a moment to reflect on your own soul. Imagine it as a translucent white light in your chest—an eternal flame of the self.

You—body and soul—are part of the infinite order of the universe—the eternal cycle of life. Perhaps you are a pragmatist … then remember that you are also made of the dust of stars and eventually you will return to it.

Whatever your core beliefs about the mystery of the world, consider yourself as part of that mystery. Imagine this: the inside of your mind is a microcosm of the universe. You will never know your own subconscious fully, nor were you meant to.

Pilgrimage teaches us to enjoy our dreams and live in the moment. It teaches us the reality of the living spirit in all of us.

Feel the breath of life and blow light out into the world.

*Every soul is destined to be perfect.*

SWAMI VIVEKANANDA (1863–1902),
SOUL, GOD, AND RELIGION

# your soul's image

A mandala is a visual metaphor of a spiritual journey, situation, or state. By using pictures cut out of magazines, your own drawings, or photographs—whatever appropriate imagery you can find—you can create a mandala of your own inner pilgrimage.

Draw a circle about 8 in (20 cm) in diameter. Divide it into four quadrants with a smaller circle at the center, as shown in the diagram. Add your own set of images to each quadrant. Treat each quadrant as one of the stages of the journey and the central circle as the sanctuary of your soul.

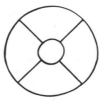

You can keep the completed mandala in the pocket at the beginning of this chapter and take it out whenever you want to remind yourself of your spiritual journey.

# the pilgrim's journal

You have reached your goal and now you are exploring your destination. You are investigating the byways and alleys of the golden city that is at the end of your journey. It is not enough simply to arrive there and leave—you must look around you and absorb the splendors of the place.

**While you are on your pilgrimage:**
• Take some exercise every day.
• Eat well and dream well.
• Take a little time every day to clear your mind. Enjoy solitude.
• Keep your spirit open to chance—pay attention.
• Exercise your imagination—trust the images that arrive from your unconscious and follow the labyrinth of your mind.

*What wondrous life is this I lead!*
*Ripe apples drop about my head;*
*The luscious clusters of the vine*
*Upon my mouth do crush their wine:*
*The nectarine and curious peach*
*Into my hands themselves do reach*
*Stumbling on melons as I pass*
*Ensnared with flowers, I fall on grass.*

ANDREW MARVELL (1621–78), THE GARDEN

Imagine arriving at the holy place. You walk up a short flight of steps and through two huge doors.

*What do you see?*

Lord, thou hast been our refuge:
from one generation to another.
Before the mountains were brought
forth, or ever the earth and the
world were made: thou art God from
everlasting, and world without end.

PSALMS, PSALM 90

The journey has been a long one. Indulge in a leisurely bath, pamper yourself, and rest your weary limbs. Allow your mind to drift to heaven.

Imagine three people conversing on the steps of the holy place. They greet you as a fellow pilgrim.

*What more do they say to you?*

*List your three greatest qualities. How can you share them?*

Go to the park, watch the children play, the ducks dive, the flowers blooming. You are blooming, too.

*Man is but earth; 'tis true; but earth is the centre. That man who dwells upon himself, who is always conversant in himself, rests in his true centre.*

JOHN DONNE (1572–1631), SERMONS

Give something freely today, expecting nothing in return.

*What can you contribute to the world or to your community?*

*The good is the beautiful.*

PLATO (429–347BC), LYSIS

*What is the connection between the stars and their reflection on the dark sea?*

*If you were an angel, who would you bless?*

*What does the word infinite mean to you? Can you remember when you first heard it?*

*At last, however, comes the full blaze of
light, in which this little self is seen to
have become one with the Infinite. Man
himself is transfigured in the presence
of this light of love, and he realizes at
last the beautiful and inspiring truth that
love, the lover, and the beloved are one.*

SWAMI VIVEKANANDA (1863–1902), PARA-BHAKTI

You are in a golden plaza, surrounded by beautiful happy people. You feel quite at home.

You are all dancing together. When the dancing stops, five children bring you gifts.

*What are they?*

*What does the word God mean to you?*

# the pilgrim's journal

You have reached your goal and now you are exploring your destination. You are investigating the byways and alleys of the golden city that is at the end of your journey. It is not enough simply to arrive there and leave—you must look around you and absorb the splendors of the place.

**While you are on your pilgrimage:**
• Take some exercise every day.
• Eat well and dream well.
• Take a little time every day to clear your mind. Enjoy solitude.
• Keep your spirit open to chance—pay attention.
• Exercise your imagination—trust the images that arrive from your unconscious and follow the labyrinth of your mind.

*What wondrous life is this I lead!*
*Ripe apples drop about my head;*
*The luscious clusters of the vine*
*Upon my mouth do crush their wine:*
*The nectarine and curious peach*
*Into my hands themselves do reach*
*Stumbling on melons as I pass*
*Ensnared with flowers, I fall on grass.*

ANDREW MARVELL (1621–78), THE GARDEN

Imagine arriving at the holy place. You walk up a short flight of steps and through two huge doors.

*What do you see?*

The journey has been a long one. Indulge in a leisurely bath, pamper yourself, and rest your weary limbs. Allow your mind to drift to heaven.

Imagine three people conversing on the steps of the holy place. They greet you as a fellow pilgrim.

*What more do they say to you?*

*List your three greatest qualities. How can you share them?*

Go to the park, watch the children play, the ducks dive, the flowers blooming. You are blooming, too.

*Man is but earth; 'tis true; but earth is the centre. That man who dwells upon himself, who is always conversant in himself, rests in his true centre.*

JOHN DONNE (1572–1631), SERMONS

Give something freely today, expecting nothing in return.

*What can you contribute to the world or to your community?*

*The good is the beautiful.*

PLATO (429–347BC), LYSIS

*What is the connection between the stars and their reflection on the dark sea?*

*If you were an angel, who would you bless?*

*What does the word infinite mean to you? Can you remember when you first heard it?*

*At last, however, comes the full blaze of
light, in which this little self is seen to
have become one with the Infinite. Man
himself is transfigured in the presence
of this light of love, and he realizes at
last the beautiful and inspiring truth that
love, the lover, and the beloved are one.*

SWAMI VIVEKANANDA (1863–1902), PARA-BHAKTI

You are in a golden plaza, surrounded by beautiful happy people. You feel quite at home.

You are all dancing together. When the dancing stops, five children bring you gifts.

*What are they?*

*What does the word God mean to you?*

# the road home

Now it is time to go home. Take what you have learned about yourself back with you. But on your return journey, don't make the mistake of picking up all the troubles and self-doubt that you have left behind. You may find that you have to make a conscious effort not to slip back into old habits of thinking and being.

**Your pilgrimage is over—but the journey continues:**
- Take the return route as slowly as you like.
- Take back a little of the food you found in the holy place.
- Take a little time every day to clear your mind.
- Keep your spirit open to chance—look out for endings and new beginnings.
- Exercise your imagination.

*To finish the moment, to find the journey's end in every step of the road, to live the greatest number of good hours, is wisdom.*

RALPH WALDO EMERSON (1803–82), EXPERIENCE

It is time to re-read the pilgrimage journal. Take your time doing this. Relive the good bits.

*How have you changed?*

*What have you learned about yourself?*

*What are you going to do differently from now on?*

*After ecstasy, the laundry.*

BUDDHIST SAYING

First published in 2003
in the United Kingdom by
Ryland Peters & Small
Kirkman House
12–14 Whitfield Street
London W1T 2RP

and in the USA by
Ryland Peters & Small, Inc.
519 Broadway
5th Floor
New York, NY 10012
www.rylandpeters.com

Writer & editorial consultant
Christina Rodenbeck

Text, design, and photographs
© Ryland Peters & Small 2003

10 9 8 7 6 5 4 3 2 1

ISBN 1 84172 519 6

Printed and bound in China.

R Y L A N D

P E T E R S

& S M A L L

LONDON   NEW YORK

# acknowledgments and credits

**Acknowledgments**

Every effort has been made to
contact copyright holders. In
the event of inadvertent error
or omission, please notify
Ryland Peters & Small. The
following writers, publishers,
and literary representatives
are thanked for permission
to use copyright material:

Lao Tzu, two excerpts from
*Tao Te Ching*, translated by
D.C. Lau (Penguin Classics,
1963), copyright © D.C. Lau
1963. Reprinted by permission
of Penguin Books Ltd.

Rachel Carson, two excerpts
from *The Sense of Wonder*
(Harper & Row, New York,
1956). Reprinted by
permission of Pollinger Ltd.

Robert Frost, excerpt from
"The Road Not Taken" from *The
Poetry of Robert Frost* edited
by Edward Connery Lathem,
The Estate of Robert Frost and
Jonathan Cape as publisher;
copyright © 1916, 1969 by
Henry Holt & Company,
copyright © 1944 by Robert
Frost. Reprinted by permission
of the Random House Group
Ltd and Henry Holt and
Company, LLC, New York.

Ehsan Yarshater (ed.), two
excerpts from *The Mystical
Poems of Rumi 2*, translated
by A.J. Arberry, copyright
© University of Chicago Press
1991. Reprinted by permission
of University of Chicago Press.

Joseph Campbell, excerpt
from *The Hero's Journey*.
Reprinted by permission of
New World Library, Novato,
CA 94949,
www.newworldlibrary.com.

**Photography credits**

Caroline Arber
Pages 60, 142.

Jan Baldwin
Pages 3, 6, 20, 21, 24, 25,
28, 29, 31, 32, 33, 34, 35,
38, 39, 40, 42, 43, 45, 47, 51,
52, 57, 61, 66, 69, 70, 71, 87,
88, 100, 101, 102, 107, 110,
111, 112, 113, 114, 115, 130,
132, 136, 137.

Christopher Drake
Page 138.

Melanie Eclare
Pages 2, 17, 22, 36, 41, 46,
53, 67, 84, 96, 97, 99, 104,
105, 106, 120, 124, 126,
127, 128, 133, 141.

Catherine Gratwicke
Page 15.

Caroline Hughes
Pages 62, 63.

Tom Leighton
Page 9.

James Merrell
Pages 4, 12, 13, 58, 79.

Pia Tryde
Pages 5, 11, 85.

Chris Tubbs
Pages 1, 10, 14, 16, 18, 19,
23, 27, 30, 37, 48, 49, 54, 55,
56, 64, 65, 72, 73, 76, 77,
80, 86, 89, 91, 92, 93, 94, 95,
103, 108, 117, 121, 123, 125,
129, 134, 135, 139, 143, 144.

Simon Upton
Pages 7, 75, 78, 81, 82, 83,
90, 109, 116.

Polly Wreford
Pages 44, 59, 68, 118, 119,
131, 140.

**Location credits**

Page 5
Ash pergola in the garden of
Dean Riddle, New York, PO Box
294, Phoenicia, NY 12464.

Page 17
Fovant Hut Garden created
by garden designer Christina
Oates together with her
husband Nigel; open to the
public. Secret Garden Designs
+44 (0)1722 714756
www.secretgardendesigns.co.uk.

Pages 22, 96, 120, 126
Sticky Wicket wildlife garden
designed and created by
Peter and Pam Lewis.
Garden Design, Restoration
& Management
+44 (0)1300 345476.

Page 124
Marc Schoellen's garden
in Luxembourg called 'La
Bergerie'
+352 327 269.

Page 128
Laura Cooper and Nick
Taggart's Los Angeles
garden, designed by
Cooper/Taggart Designs
+1 323 256 3048
coopertaggart@earthlink.net.

Pages 133, 141
The garden and nursery De
Brinkhof of Riet Brinkhof
and Joop Van Den Berk.
De Brinkhof Garden & Nursery,
The Netherlands
+31 487 531 486.